Zookeepers

Focus: Careers

Meredith Costain

Zookeepers take care of animals in zoos.

Zookeepers take care of big animals and baby animals.

Zookeepers make meals
for the animals.

Zookeepers feed
the animals.

Zookeepers clean the animals.

Zookeepers clean the animals' homes.

Zookeepers play with
the animals, too!